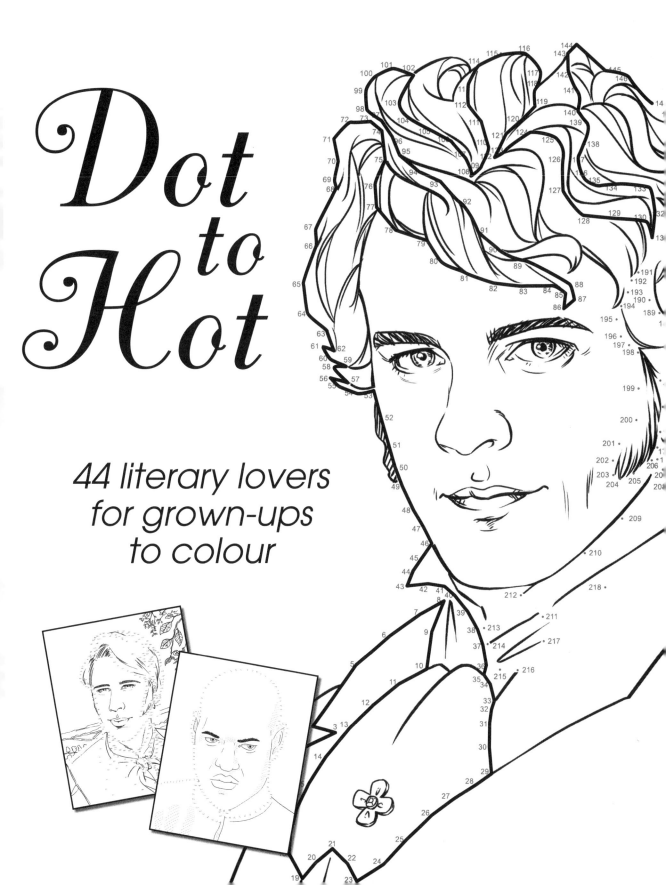

Dot to Hot

44 literary lovers for grown-ups to colour

It is a truth universally acknowledged that a romantic person in possession of a good set of colouring pencils must be in want of a Dot-to-Hot book!

This book is simply bursting with dot-to-dot heart-throbs from Heathcliff to Mr Darcy.

From heroes and romantics to rebels and villains, these literary lovers and bad boys are all waiting to be lovingly completed by you!

Angel Clare

Tess of the d'Urbervilles

Angel is romance personified. He strides around offering to carry dairy maids over swollen streams. He's a dreamer, an idealist. When this farmer meets Tess the milkmaid they fall in love. Tess is beautiful, Angel's love is pure. Angel thinks they'll have a beautiful farming life together, doing things like lambing and May dances and other things like threshing (which sounds like quite hard work).

What could possibly go wrong? He abandons Tess ON THEIR WEDDING NIGHT, decides to go to Brazil and asks one of his wife's best friends to come with him on a whim, as his mistress. How is this ok? It's not! Eventually he comes back for Tess but by then it's all far, far too late and the whole thing ends in tragedy. So yes, Angel Clare might sound dreamy, but he's actually as romantic as a cow pat. Stay clear.

Fitzwilliam Darcy

Pride and Prejudice

If you have high standards, like vast country estates in Derbyshire
and don't mind a ferociously snobbish aunt and massive sideburns
(Darcy's, not the aunt's), then this is the man for you. It will help if
you possess: a pair of fine eyes; wit; a teasing, playful manner; a desire
to be loved ardently; and an embarrassing mother. Just try a little
singing at the pianoforte, dip your petticoats in some mud
and turn him down first, at least twice.

Treat him mean basically – it works like a dream.

Edward Rochester

Jane Eyre

Darkly romantic… but if you like that sort of thing, remember to ask how *dark* you want to go. Secret wife hidden in the attic? So mad she'll come into your bedroom at night and stare at you as you sleep? A guy who will cross-dress as a fortune teller to find out what you're thinking? You might think that's going a little too far. But don't forget that Mr Rochester does passion (we're talking deep passion here) and TRUE LOVE. He's unsmiling, complex, wounded, tortured. At times brutally cruel, at other times amazingly tender. He'll save a woman from a burning building, love you for being yourself and call for you across windswept moors.

This is a man with all consuming romantic hero power – turbo-charged. "I am coming," you'll reply. "Wait for me! Oh, I will come!"

Arthur Clennam

Little Dorrit

Do you yearn for 'Quietly Ever After'? Then Arthur's your man.
He's the opposite of what you'd expect from a hero. He's passive.
He's frequently ineffectual. At 40, he is (by the standards of his time)
middle-aged, with no money and no prospects. But he's also kind,
loyal and generous. He overcomes a cold, deprived, unloving,
generally horrible childhood to become an unsung hero, determined
to make amends for any harm his father may have caused.

He's good without being moralistic. He's lonely and a little lost.
His love story is sweet and selfless. One, two, three... awww.

Rawdon Crawley

Vanity Fair

This six foot cavalry officer starts out as a pool hustler and a card shark, who is always looking for a way to avoid paying his bills. He's not exactly a stranger to violence; he is always up for a duel. But he's a rake that's reformed by love and turns into a doting, domesticated husband and father. Well-meaning, but no match for his calculating, sharp-witted wife.

It's actually quite hard to imagine him as a hero when all you want to do is take pity on him. Think tough guy gone mushy.

Tom Jones

The History of Tom Jones, a Foundling

Unbridled, hot-tempered, saucy and sexy, Tom is 200 years before his time, and all the better for it. He jumps from bed to bed, free and easy, having glorious, lusty fun. More importantly, he does it all without disrespecting women.

He's gallant, the old-fashioned way. One of the few romantic heroes to think he might have slept with his mother by mistake (luckily his real mother turned out to be someone else). Often foolish, he gets things wrong, but makes amends and is ultimately prepared to change his wild ways for his TRUE LOVE.

He's rollicking. He's frolicking. Consider turning into a bawdy eighteenth century wench for a night of fun with Tom.

Totally worth the time travel.

Inspector Javert

Les Misérables

Javert hunts down criminals like a bloodhound following a scent. He's stern, inflexible and devoted to his job – the epitome of a good cop.

Strong, determined, dark and brooding. A single-minded man of action, unlikely ever to get emotional. He'd undoubtedly be great in emergency situations. Maybe not so good at relationships, remembering birthdays and little things like feelings.

Least likely to say: "Darling, I'm having some trouble expressing my emotions. Shall we go to couples therapy?"
Most likely to say: "My life's not worth living if I can't do my job."

Theodore Laurence

Little Women

The classic boy-next-door, Laurie is handsome, smiling and charming.
If that sounds bland, don't forget he's also strong-willed, quick-tempered
and adventurous. Add to that mix the fact that he's half-Italian and
combines youth, passion and privilege. He sounds like a dream. For the
icing on the cake, he's deliciously rich yet down-to-earth and is capable
of heroic deeds such as saving the drowning Amy from an icy river.

Perfect, right? No! Because he goes and marries the WRONG SISTER.
How could he? Laurie is meant to marry Jo. NOT Amy. Ok, so Jo
turned him down, but still. He shouldn't have gone gallivanting
around Europe and then fallen for her prissy, irritating younger sister.
So, so wrong. Laurie, what were you thinking? You let us all down.
You should feel ashamed.

Ross Poldark

Poldark

Move over Mr Darcy. Romantic, wronged, brooding, introspective, broken-hearted, Ross Poldark has it all. Poldark isn't just good-looking, he's also GOOD. He stands up for poachers, helps fugitives, fights cheats. He's troubled and argumentative; he can be found gaming and drinking but he's never cruel. This man gives good reason to hotfoot it down to a Cornish clifftop, just in case you can catch a glimpse of him riding around on horseback, preferably with his shirt off, displaying his well-toned chest. Ok, so this might be slightly confusing the book and the TV series… but either way, like a prince from a fairy tale, he rescues a girl from poverty and sets about saving his small corner of the world.

So swoonsome, it makes it seem worthwhile becoming a servant and changing your name to Demelza.

Othello

Othello

Eloquent, broad-shouldered, muscular, powerful,
a man who loves deeply and madly.
And in the end, mainly madly.

He goes from hot, loving husband to insane
jealousy and then, oh yes, murder. So maybe
think twice before hooking up with an insecure
general in insidious Venice. Especially one
who listens to lies about you. And trusts a
guy who brands himself 'Honest Iago' (anyone
who does that is SO OBVIOUSLY a massive liar).

And above all, avoid being seen with handsome
younger men called Cassio. It won't end well.

Heathcliff

Wuthering Heights

Dark skinned with eyes full of black fire, Heathcliff is Byronic,
brooding and enigmatic. His incredible loyalty in love is
rather offset by his evil urge to destroy his entire foster family.
Not for the faint-hearted and possibly easier to idealise during
hormone-soaked teenage years than when reading about
him with a nice cup of tea while you ponder a crossword.

Romantic? Yes. Mentally unstable, sadistic, obsessive?
Oh yes. Something slightly, er, supernatural about him?
It's been hinted at. And quite hard to imagine him helping
out with the Sunday roast or the school run.

Charles Bingley

Pride and Prejudice

Your mum loves him. He laughs at her terrible jokes.
Your dad loves him. They hang out. Your sisters love him.
He's gently flirtatious and always spontaneously
putting on balls. "Bit bored today?" he'll say.
"Pon rep! Let's have a ball."

Basically, everyone loves Bingley. But maybe
you're wondering if he's just a little bit, um, dull?
All that affability and small talk is potentially quite
annoying. He's so easily led you could probably get
him to waltz naked through Meryton, wearing a
bonnet and singing a mildly saucy sea shanty.

Darkest moment: being too modest to believe Jane has
really fallen in love with him. If it's an alpha male you're
after, this is the wrong suitor for your hand. But if you
want rich, handsome and placid, he's perfect.

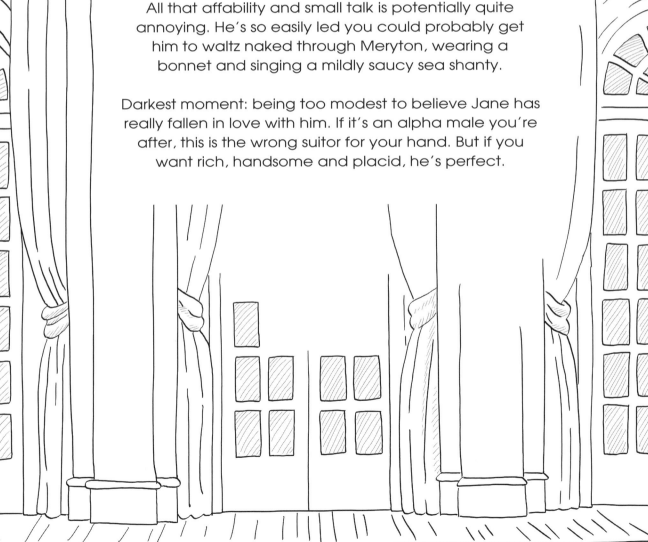

Captain Frederick Wentworth

Persuasion

He writes possibly the greatest love letter in the entire history of great love letters. "You pierce my soul. I am half agony, half hope. Tell me not that I am too late…" He's handsome, he's charming, he's self-made rather than entitled. He's constant and true but... HE MAKES ANNE WAIT FOR HIM FOR EIGHT YEARS!

Eight years is a long time. Ok, so she dumped him first, but he didn't have to go larking around with Louisa Musgrove, or insult Anne's appearance. And he's really bad at communicating. But then we come back to THAT letter: "I have loved none but you. Unjust I may have been, weak and resentful I have been, but never inconstant."

Take him back, Anne. All is forgiven. Eight years is nothing. We're rooting for you, Frederick!

Frank Churchill

Emma

Handsome, charming, great at letter writing and everyone talks about him ALL THE TIME. You wait your whole life to meet him and then when you finally do… OBVIOUSLY you're going to fall for him. Even though there's a little whisper, like a fairy-sized maiden aunt in your ear, saying "isn't he just a tiny bit flaky in the flesh? A tad metrosexual, maybe? He's definitely had his teeth done…". But you ignore that little voice because he's SO good at banter (and frankly you're a little bored with your life) and you start ignoring your old friends and laughing at harmless old biddies to impress him… and then it turns out he was SECRETLY ENGAGED all along!

Yes, you've got it. He's a two-timing rat. His one redeeming feature is fixing an old granny's glasses. Stay clear.

Edward Ferrars

Sense and Sensibility

Loves one woman; tied to another. Clumsy, bumbling, inarticulate.
Reticent, passive, dutiful. Not handsome, but honourable. If it's thrusting
ambition you want, look away. Ed yearns only for a life of peaceful
domesticity. His name is never going to be writ large in the 'Top Ten
Greatest Heroes of All Time'. But he's actually been massively under
appreciated. Buried beneath his diffidence, there's the tender heart,
the kindness. And when you stop to think about it, he'd be lovely
to snuggle up with on the sofa on a Sunday night.

He'd watch 'The Great British Bake Off' with you and make wry
comments about cake. He'd bring you hot honey and lemon if you had
the flu and take out the rubbish, without ever being asked. Think of him
as 'the quiet hero'; the literary equivalent of a warm, fluffy blanket.

Henry Tilney

Northanger Abbey

Witty, clever, lively and sarcastic, Henry can even give good chat on chick lit novels, or what makes a good muslin. Ok, so he's a tiny bit patronising, mocks others' naiveté and there's a touch of Henry Higgins about him, but that doesn't have to be a bad thing. His high point? Not judging Catherine when she confesses that she thought his father MURDERED his mother. Obviously this could be quite an awkward moment in the path of true love, but he lets it pass.

Teasing, playful and urbane, Henry could easily glide out of his faux gothic romance on to a quiz show panel.

George Wickham

Pride and Prejudice

Think the regency Prince Harry, but without the cash – a hot army boy
who chats you up, gets you drunk at parties, ignores your calls
and then dumps you for an heiress.

He lies and he cheats and will definitely leave town without paying
his debts. So don't lend him your wallet. Or your younger sister.
Or introduce him to any rich friends. If you don't want to fall for him,
try not to see him in uniform or on horseback. And definitely not
both at the same time. If you find you can't resist…
just remember – you were warned.

Pip Pirrip

Great Expectations

Orphan boy, Pip, meets orphan girl, Estella, in the crumbling mansion owned by a deranged old spinster, and is exhorted to love her. Only unfortunately for Pip, Estella is being groomed to be cold, distant, aloof and HEARTLESS. Bit twisted? Definitely. Does Pip fall for it? Absolutely.

He loves Estella obsessively, even turning to snobbery and greed in his desperate quest to become a wealthy gentleman and win her.

So you'd think that we don't really love Pip and don't really want them to get together... but we do! Because whatever Pip's flaws are, at heart he is kind and compassionate. We want what he wants – so much so that Dickens was forced to re-write the ending so that they *can* live happily ever after. You can't say things like "You are part of my existence, part of myself" and NOT have people rooting for you.

Benedick Mountanto

Much Ado About Nothing

Hey nonny nonny… if the game of love is a war of words,
then Benedick is the master. He can banter, flirt and tease
but is never caught. Arrogant and taunting, he rails against
marriage, but for all his bravado, he falls
into a love trap like a ripe plum.

So he only wants to outsmart and out-insult Beatrice?
Except when he thinks Beatrice loves him, it only takes
a moment for him to fall headlong in love with her. He
changes from a man's man to one who is prepared to fight
his friend to prove his love. Go Benedick, proto-feminist!

Falling for him and relishing his witty wooing is a bit like
swooning over your English teacher – makes you feel
clever and warm all at the same time.

Sergeant Frank Troy

Far from the Madding Crowd

Cocky alpha male, total player, handsome, vain and highly irresponsible.
For example, he refuses to marry Fanny Robin, the love of his life, just
because she turns up at the wrong church (easy mistake to make).
As a result, Fanny dies while he's shacked up with Bathsheba (who isn't
having such a great time either, having discovered that Frank SHOCK
HORROR doesn't really care for farming). Only after Fanny's tragic death
does Frank start to feel sorry for her. Well, it's a bit late by then, isn't it
Frank? Give us Gabriel Oak and his amazing sheep bloat skills any day.

Greatest moment: wooing Bathsheba with a private display of
swordsmanship. Chapter 28 'The Hollow Amid the Ferns'
is DEFINITELY worth a read.

3 •
2 •
1 •

Colonel Brandon

Sense and Sensibility

He likes flannel waistcoats and complains of a touch of rheumatism in one of his shoulders. He is silent, reserved, serious, old before his time. There is NOTHING sexy about Colonel Brandon. But there is everything to love about him. He is patient, devoted, sincere and above all, good. For him, there are no wild words or empty gestures. He is a true hero.

A chivalrous, selfless, devoted knight. Any sensible woman would choose Brandon. To love a Brandon is the path to future joy. Here's a mantra to be repeated daily: must fall for Brandon, not Willoughby. Brandon not Willoughby. Oh but Willoughby is so fun and sexy. Willoughby would never wear flannel waistcoats. Argh. Brandon, not Willoughby, Brandon not Willoughby! I bet Brandon irons his pants. And sleeps with his mouth open. No, no, mustn't get distracted. Brandon, not Willoughby, Brandon NOT Willoughby…!

Hawkeye

The Last of the Mohicans

Seriously hardcore man of the forest. Makes all other men look like soppy puppies. Has some awesome nicknames: Natty Bumppo, La Longue Carabine (The Long Rifle), The Scout. Loyal to his friends, he could guide you safely through the wilderness and has insane rifle skills. He even dresses up as a bear. Convincingly.

Hawkeye is basically Superman in buckskin leggings and a fur cap. You'd definitely want him around if you were stuck up a tree, being hunted by a mountain lion or if you're just generally into heroic Tarzan types (plus gun). Does appear to be celibate for the ENTIRE novel, but no matter. Maybe brush up on your tracking skills, marksmanship and wilderness chat and you've bagged yourself a hero.

Oberon

A Midsummer Night's Dream

Oberon – King of the Fairies – also a bit of a ladies' man. He may be married to the Fairy Queen, but that hasn't stopped him having a string of torrid affairs, including Hippolyta, his 'warrior love'. He even disguised himself as a shepherd so he could hook up with a country girl called Phillida. (From now on, beware of shepherds – may actually be randy Fairy Kings in disguise).

He thinks romance is a bit of a sport, sometimes for the good, like helping blundering humans back on their path to happiness. Sometimes, not so good… like when he sprinkles love juice in his wife's eyes so that she falls in love with a donkey. What an ass.

John Thornton

North and South

A hero who doesn't just sit around in tight pantaloons but is a
MAN OF ACTION, building factories, running factories, and generally
being a gallant factory owner. He also does brooding very well.
Approximately 70% of his time is spent brooding (whilst simultaneously
being a MAN OF ACTION). The other 30% is given over
to revealing his INNER DEPTHS (learning, growing,
developing compassion, falling in love etc.).

And he falls in love so well. He falls hard and true and doesn't give up,
with a little bit of tortured pride and misunderstanding thrown in.
John Thornton is to heroes what tea is to the biscuit world.
Indispensable. Lucky, lucky Margaret Hale.

Brom Van Brunt

The Legend of Sleepy Hollow

Strong, rough, manly, great on horseback and the hero of the countryside. Full of vim and vigour, he's also a bit of a trickster who definitely wins the competition of 'How Far Would You Go to Get the Girl?' in the small town of Sleepy Hollow. He's prepared to dress up as the ghost of the Headless Horseman (with the help of a pumpkin) and hang around tree stumps at night, freaking the life out of his love rival.

We're not talking complex, tortured character here – more high school prankster up for a laugh. Kind of like Loki crossed with Thor crossed with a cowboy. Maybe fun and attractive if you're a teenager and into dating clichéd alpha males.

Henry Crawford

Mansfield Park

It's a classic love story: a popular, handsome boy tries to make a nerdy girl fall for him, only to truly fall for her and discover she won't have him. So he sets out to prove his love and win her hand. It could have been one of the greatest love stories of all time... except the boy goes and ruins it.

He heads to London, meets an ex and can't resist wooing her back. Their adulterous affair ends in a massive scandal and his social ruin. Henry Crawford – you so nearly had it all – sexy, funny, sparkling, seductive... if only you weren't so weak and vain. A playboy who never grew up. You're probably wandering the streets of London still, consoling yourself with a drink and your smart phone.

James Steerforth

David Copperfield

He's the most popular boy in school – the one that gets everything he wants, just the way he wants it. The guy you'd be desperate to be friends with, even though he'd steal your tuck money and laugh about you, just to make himself look good. But then you'd think it's ok because he's so brilliant, charming and talented.

Well, heed the warning signs! Like the fact his mother's companion has a scar on her face from where he threw a hammer at her. So it's not entirely surprising when he runs off with Little Em'ly and then cruelly abandons her. Steerforth is also shallow, egotistical and, in the end, totally irredeemable.

Long John Silver

Treasure Island

A cunning and opportunistic pirate with an intelligent, smiling
face, who is also courageous, masterful and charismatic.
So hot, you're drawn to him even though he has a PARROT
ON HIS SHOULDER who says "pieces of eight" a lot.

Ok, he is also a villain who commits cold-blooded murder,
but he's so brilliantly complex and colourful you can't help
hoping he'll escape at the end to sail the seas once more.
Which is wrong, of course, but Silver IS the pirate to end all pirates.

Dr Henry Jekyll

The Strange Case of Dr Jekyll and Mr Hyde

He's a popular, intelligent scientist, known for his highbrow dinner parties and charitable works. He is widely liked and well-respected. He seems so good – a great catch on the Victorian marriage market.

Except... he's actually two people; the good Dr Jekyll and the bad Mr Hyde, whom he created by concocting a home-made potion. So more like buy one, get one free; two for the price of one. Which might be fun, except Mr Hyde is completely evil and depraved and has a tendency to leap out from Dr Jekyll whenever he's having a quiet snooze and then rush around being seriously perverted and murdering people.

Basically, he's a sociopath whose dark side puts Heathcliff to shame.

Daniel Deronda

Daniel Deronda

Brilliant, idealistic and lost, Daniel doesn't know who he truly is, where he comes from or where he's going. Really good at saving people, from poor students and young women trying to drown themselves to fair beauties called Gwendolen in need of lots of advice. Fancy some help? Dan's the man. Earnest and soul-searching, selfless and intelligent…

Trouble is, he's so stuffed full of righteousness he's quite hard to actually fall for. Unless you prefer a guy on a pedestal, radiating goodness into the world, helping you become your best self. Mildly exhausting? Yes. But if you like someone full of zest and zeal then look no further.

John Thorpe

Northanger Abbey

Thorpe is basically the biggest blustering fool in Austen's novels. He appears to be a bluffer and a bit of a buffoon. He loves a pint down the pub and a chat about horses. Slightly prone to yelling and swearing but seems pretty harmless.

But underneath that blustering exterior, Thorpe is also a calculating villain. He'll never admit he's wrong about anything, even when he's caught in an outright lie. He misleads, he tricks and at one point, he even resorts to kidnapping (if you count not letting someone out of your carriage as kidnapping).

WARNING: this man is not a hero. Even Jane Austen was rude about him.

John Willoughby

Sense and Sensibility

First sprain your ankle. (Sprained ankles are great for picking up men
in literary fiction. The pain is totally worth it.) It will also help if it's raining
and you're within carrying distance of your house. Lie artfully on the
ground, waiting for handsome, gallant Willoughby to appear, so he can
swoop you up in his arms and clutch you to his broad, manly chest.
A faint blush will spread across your cheeks, you will mumble your
thanks but he won't leave before promising to return
the next day to check on your condition.

It is all SO romantic. (Ok, it doesn't end well. He'll never marry you. He
may have charm but he's also weak, pleasure-seeking and selfish.)
But let's not focus on that. Let's just think about this moment;
this perfectly romantic moment.

Edmund Bertram

Mansfield Park

Edmund is the Prince Charming to Fanny Price's Cinderella – full of
kindness and gentleness. He's the only member of his family to
care for the poor little girl who comes to live with them, uprooted
from her home and family. And then, in the end, he marries her.

Perfect love story? NO. Because along the way, serious, moralistic
Edmund falls for the vivacious Mary Crawford. He steals Fanny's pony
so he can go riding with Mary, leaves her sitting alone and forlorn
on a bench while he gallivants around a garden and ultimately
only comes back to Fanny when he realises Mary's true nature.
Also, they are FIRST COUSINS! So, so wrong.

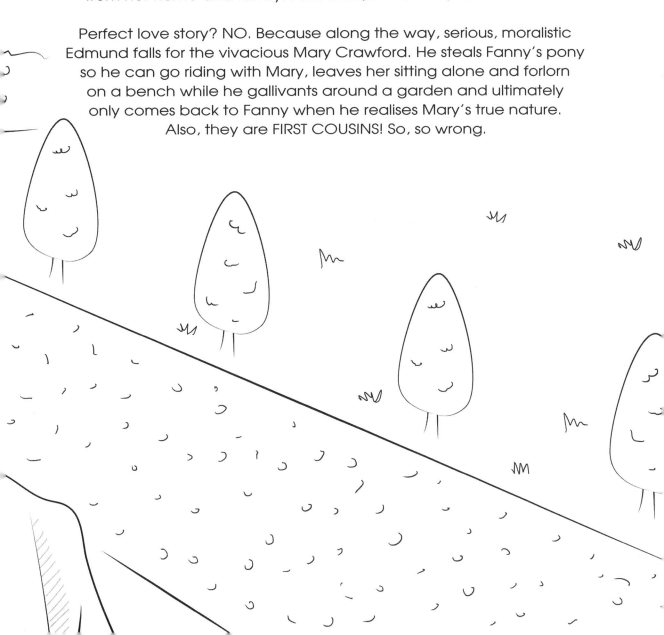

George Knightley

Emma

Not brooding, or dark, or moody. No inconvenient ex-wives locked in his attic or burning fires of resentment. Mr Knightley is the PERFECT gentleman. He's got a massive house and loads of money, but doesn't flash his cash. He's kind to loquacious old ladies. He dances with wallflowers. He'll even move in to keep your curmudgeonly dad happy. Ok, so he might tell you off if you're rude/prone to matchmaking, but in a sexy school teacher way. He's the kind of guy who would always have a really big umbrella to hand when it rains. This one's a keeper.

Just don't call him 'Knightley' (very vulgar). It's 'Mr Knightley' or, after twenty years of marriage, you might feel ready to venture on to 'George'.

Tybalt Capulet

Romeo and Juliet

Very handy with a sword. A macho, aggressive, gang-leader style
swaggering alpha male. Not a bad person to have on your side in a
fight and incredibly loyal to his family. Surprisingly, he's also a bit of
a pro at rhyming couplets. Pretty much every time he opens
his mouth, they pop out, perfectly formed.

If he sounds a bit shallow, consider the fact that he's quite possibly
secretly and massively in love with his cousin, Juliet, and is prepared to
beat anyone up who comes near her, which you could take as romantic
in a slightly twisted, hot-heated kind of way. Unfortunately, like Romeo,
he also ends up dead, which seems to be par for the course
if you live in a Veronese rhyming romantic tragedy.

Edmond Dantès

The Count of Monte Cristo

A naive and innocent sailor turns to vengeance after being wrongfully imprisoned. But his revenge is done with flair, imagination and resourcefulness.

Sinbad the Sailor, Abbé Busoni and Lord Wilmore… they're all disguises adopted by the mysterious, fabulously rich aristocrat, the Count of Monte Cristo (another disguise). Confusing? A little. But if you like your heroes cold and complex, with the possibility of being ultimately reformed by true love, then the Count is your man.

There is the scary dedication to revenge (he waits for YEARS) but no matter. The important thing is 'to wait and hope'.

Romeo Montague

Romeo and Juliet

Impulsive, rash, prone to daydreaming about love... A LOT. Great at climbing up balconies, hiding from Nurse and making swoonsome speeches about stars, suns and wanting to be a glove against his True Love's cheek (a really underrated dating technique. Why does no one do that anymore?). He has a slight problem with fate. It tends to catch up with him. He misses important messages (not exactly his fault, but it doesn't end well) and has a tendency to kill people in the heat of the moment, one of whom happens to be his TRUE LOVE's favourite cousin. Redeeming features? Clearly hot, handsome, ardent, totally romantic but sadly, by the end, dead.

Andrei Bolkonsky

War and Peace

First up, he's a prince. An actual prince. Woo hoo!
But not a layabout prince – a noble one.

As soon as war breaks out, he rushes off to enlist, to prove himself.
Slightly less heroically, he leaves behind his heavily pregnant
wife and returns just in time, to see her die in childbirth.

After that he basically turns into the Russian Darcy, cynically
sidling around the ballrooms of St. Petersburg, until he meets
Natasha and falls for her. It is a moment of GREAT ROMANCE,
ending in EVEN GREATER TRAGEDY when she betrays him.
He forgives her, and then dies in her arms from
yet more war wounds.

#sonoble #weloveyouandrei #hotprince

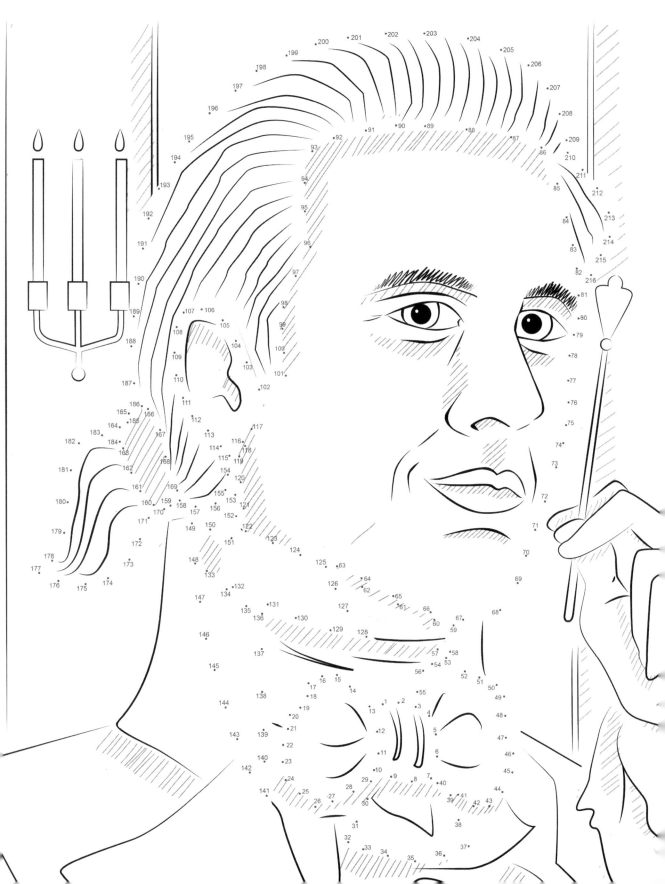

Sir Percy Blakeney

The Scarlet Pimpernel

Is Sir Percy Blakeney just a dull, slow-witted foppish bore who minces around ballrooms and does nothing but raise his quizzing glass and his perfectly arched eyebrows? You may think so, but you would be so, so wrong. Our Percy is also a master of disguise, slipping into France to rescue aristocrats from the guillotine whilst also being incredibly witty and good at repartee.

Percy AKA the Scarlet Pimpernel is so romantic he puts Romeo to shame. Here's why Percy is so hot: noble – yes; quick-witted – yes; amazing at swordplay – yes; devoted to his wife – yes; has a secret identity – yes; has his own league – yes; looks good in tight pantaloons – oh yes.

What's not to love? Why don't they make them like this anymore? Where is he when you need him in the Tinder-infested twenty-first century? That demned elusive Pimpernel…

King Richard

Richard III

So he's a little bit evil. Ok, so he's more than that – he's basically evil personified. He kills his nephews. He kills his brother. He kills his wife's first husband and father-in-law. He's an angry, self-absorbed, insecure maniac who is plotting to rule the world with a little bit of mass destruction, terror and murder thrown in.

Not much to like? Well, maybe… except he's SO MUCH fun. Richard is clever, suave, witty, enthralling, really good at making you laugh (at his victims) and there's just a little part of you that's rooting for him all the way. Oh, and he has serious language skills. Who cares if he is totally evil, when he makes words sing?

Professor Friedrich Bhaer

Little Women

He's poor but generous. He does GOOD DEEDS, like helping maids with coal scuttles and looking after orphan nephews. He has the kindest eyes and tousled brown hair. He can teach Shakespeare.

People are drawn to him like a warm fire. He proposes with a full heart and empty hands and his kiss under an umbrella wipes away a future of loneliness. Or, you might think he is a staid, stout, prematurely aged, deeply unromantic didactic professor, who hangs around in doorways with a darning needle and a sock, all the while creepily referring to himself as 'Old Fritz'.

So which are you? Team Bhaer or Team Laurie? You decide…

King Henry

Henry V

Ok, so in his youth he was a bit rowdy – hanging out in seedy bars with his dodgy drinking pals and taking part in the odd highway robbery. Think army boy out on the town, trying to chat you up whilst eating a kebab. But now… now he's all grown up and kingly and a TOTAL warrior hero (if you ignore the part where he betrays his old friends and threatens to murder the children of Harfleur).

But we can forgive him, because he's a KING who lived a really long time ago when that type of thing was totally fine. Also, he knows how to woo. He woos his French princess, even though he could have just demanded that she marry him after he thrashed France with a bit of longbow action. And he's as good at wooing as he is at motivational speaking, i.e. AMAZING. If it's a kingly wooer you're after, Henry's your man.

Dorian Gray

The Picture of Dorian Gray

Not just good looking but beautiful. Beautifully beautiful. And at first, Dorian is as pure and innocent as a spring lamb. So if that's the Dorian Gray you're after, stop right there, because after that he becomes hedonistic, selfish, corrupt and, yes, even murderous.

So what's the allure of Dorian Gray? Well, he's got the best anti-ageing device EVER. Better than Botox. Better than liposuction. Even beats plastic surgery. Yes, you guessed it, all his horrible depravity, sinful ways and wrinkles end up on a portrait of him, not on his face. So get with Dorian, learn his secrets, and you too could be youthful forever, (just don't be tempted to take a knife to the painting).

Marius Pontmercy

Les Misérables

He has all the qualities that make a romantic hero by the bucketload. Handsome – oh yes. Strong-willed – he chooses his own path. Brave – fighting in the barricades and risking his own life when he thinks he has lost his love. We can just pass over the part where he doesn't even notice that Eponine is desperately in love with him. Or when he bans Valjean from seeing his adopted daughter. So is he the ideal hero? Well yes, except… that's also the problem. It would be like dating an app on your phone, programmed for 'romance'. Great in theory. Really dull in reality. You sort of get the impression that if you took off all his clothes he'd be made entirely of words.

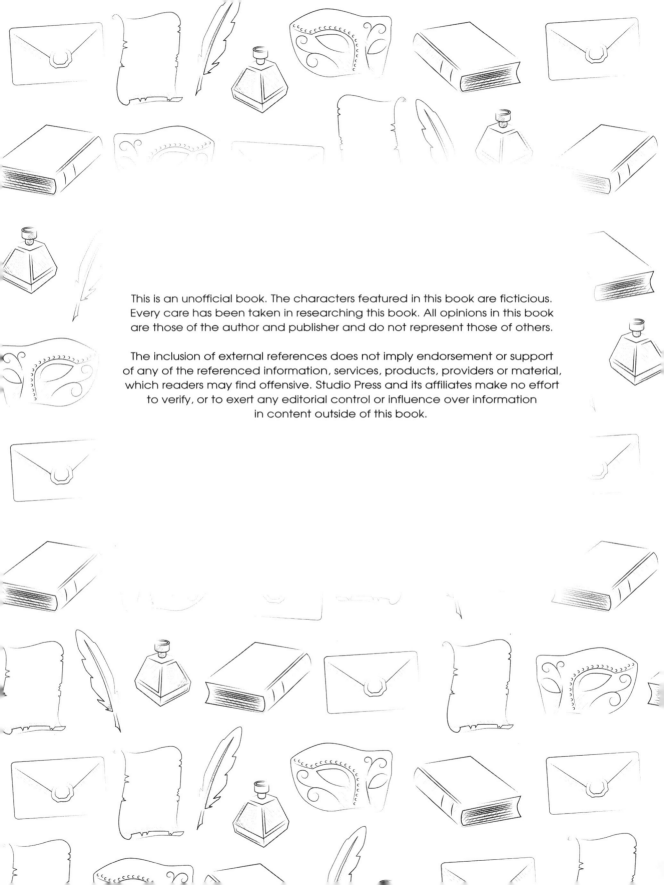